GW00716375

Essays of a Lacademic

By A.J. Ward

All the poems contained within this book are the original work of A. J. Ward and no part may be copied or reproduced without written permission from the author.

ISBN: 978-0-9561719-0-0

First published 2006
Designed, typeset and printed by
Chatterbox Publications
2 Alpine Rise
Coventry
CV3 6NT
024 7641 4458
www.chatterbox-publications.co.uk

For
Frank and Marion
without whose
D. Day celebration
this book would
never have been
possible.
And of course
Rosie and Teresa.

Contents

NATURE

Where does it come from
Is it a thing of itself
Or divinity.

It can't be made, bought,
Paid for, purchased, manufactured,
Or earned

The colours, the seasons,
The stars
Oceans, mountains, rivers,
Sunsets, morning dew.
Enjoy it all.

MUSIC

Any mood any mode
From the first drum onward
The magic of music
When you're down it lifts you up
Party with rock
Smooch under low lights
A lost loves favourite tune
A moment, a situation
Triggers a song
The joy of dance
The serenity of background
Rhythm - beat - fast - slow
A tempo for every occasion
Keep on playing

RAILWAY

We stepped off the train the first time
We didn't go to the end of the line

Chance, finds us at destiny station
Do we board a second time

Look for the signals

Do we buy one way tickets
And remain seated

Or do we step off again
To go down our separate branch lines

RIVER

Ice cold water follows the hot
Are you wary of bathing again
Are you afraid of plunging in
Even though the waters tepid

The stream trickles at the moment
Dare you step in and test the flow
Tread carefully on the pebbles
Even though the waters tepid

Is the current running faster
Do you paddle or do you swim
Do you stay out of the river
Even though the waters tepid

Blindfold

Our heads were carapaced
Inside the shell
Resentment at first sight
Seems only friends could tell

Inverted magnetism
Was hard to quell
Feelings of alienation
Seems only friends could tell

Gradually it turned around
We boarded the same carousel
That was forty years ago
Seems only friends could tell

MYSTERY

A casual glance
A brush of shoulder
A meeting of eyes that
Instantly smoulder
A friend of a friend
A shopping trolley collision
A moment in time
A lifelong decision

FRIEND

What are you for
You are for being here
You are for easing the pain
We, are for sharing the strain
You are for arguing with
We, are for agreeing with
You are for talking to
We, are for listening to
You are for making me smile
We, are for laughing a while
You give me your time
We, watch the years go by

DREAMAWAY

I long for a place of peace
Where self interested
Materialism has no room

Where the grass is
Greenest no matter
The side

Where all wear the
Boot with none underfoot

Where economy is humane
And none go without

Where

(RRRRRING)

STREETS

The man-hole cover is still there
Where the can was placed for rin-tin-tin

The entry, where we stroked
The bunny or used a dustbin lid
For cricket stumps

The corner shop, where sometimes
You could smell cigar smoke
On the sliced ham you'd bought

The house at the top of the
Next street where we knocked
On the back door to buy
Black current lollies

But childhood moves to
Adulthood and all things
Must change

Yet the atmosphere is
Still above us

Down here, there's only remains

VIEWPOINT

Mum packs the sheets
In plenty of time
We're going on holiday
To the seaside

Down to the station
Can't hardly wait
Look at the driver
The engine, the footplate

Slamming of doors
Whistle is blown
Skidding wheels grip
We judder out slow

The train picks up speed
The corridors packed
Kids sat on cases
Babies on laps

Out come the brandysnaps
Batches and pop
Collapsible beakers
Filled to the top

At last we arrive
The holiday can begin
Catch a bus to the campsite
Where Dad will sign in

We go in the chalet
Have a sit down
The Calor gas is full
So it's cuppa's all round

Up in the morning
With towel and soap
It's a walk to the washhouse
Sunny weather we hope

Then after breakfast
It's bucket and spade
Down to the beach
Sandcastles well made

Sports day is next
All the campers turn out
Sack race, egg and spoon
Hear everyone shout

Postcards sent home
Tea towels to buy
Sticks of rock too
Before its goodbye

It's over so soon
It's over so fast
Hope that next year's
As good as the last

EPOCH

Big bang of singularity
Atoms born
They gathered made dust
Matter and form
Galaxies of stars
Emitting heat and light
Nursing their children
The planets - life
Dinosaurs came
Then were gone
Annihilated by asteroid
Drowning the sun
Then something curious
Canopied forests bore
An upright inquisitive
Like nothing before
Progressive species
Traversed the land
Limitless learning
With eye and hand
This story's been told
In many format and mode
Different theories explanations
Down the same road
Are we forever to be
Chagrined the experts sigh
Finding an answer
To the simplest of questions
"Why?"

HUMAN

We are unique
At least on Earth

What other species
Has a dress sense

What else turns down
An offering
Because it's polite

Who says yes
When they mean no

Who smiles and nods
When they'd rather not

And who is it
Takes time and trouble
For others
And will give all
For a friend

SECRET

What's the secret of being a success
It's a question people ask
Is the answer in the minds recess
Is there no one to finish the task

It's a question people ask
Its been a puzzle since time began
Is there no one to finish the task
Boy, girl, woman or man

Its been a puzzle since time began
No ones made it clear
Boy, girl, woman or man
Witchdoctor, medium or seer

No ones made it clear
No ones worked it out
Witchdoctor, medium or seer
Its making me scream and shout

No ones worked it out
Is the answer in the minds recess
Its making me scream and shout
What's the secret of being a success

WALKING

Four paws plus two feet take a walk
Companions on display
Friendship by instinctive talk
Only love is the price they pay.

Companions on display
Faith in each other revealed
Only love is the price they pay
No pretence or secret concealed

Faith in each other revealed
Trust at both ends of the lead
No pretence or secret concealed
Closeness so rare guaranteed

Trust at both ends of the lead
Sensing the others concern
Closeness so rare guaranteed
A lesson for all to discern

Sensing the others concern
Friendship by instinctive talk
A lesson for all to discern
Four paws plus two feet take a walk

MOMENT

Is it luck, fate, God's will
The path set
The road made

Right place right time
Wrong place wrong time

Who, what, loads the dice cube.
Is it loaded.

Even the talented
Get a lucky throw

WALL

Can the seaside donkey rider
Ever become master of the hounds
Can the tabloider
Enjoy a hoof and bone mag
Would the supermarket shirt wearer
Feel comfortable in a wax jacket
Could the grouse shooter
Swap the double barrel for a pool cue

The space between
Is immeasurable distance
Can it be bridged
Without resistance

Can the two come together
And make amends
Or will the bumpkin and the townie
Never be friends

HOLIDAY

Outward bound the tumbrilled
Mass with half closed eyes
And faces like buckets
Peer through woods and seniors
Atop the pea soup deck

Homeward,
A cackle of excitement fills the air
The condemned now free
Joy and jollity atop the deck
Homeward bound for Monday's tea

INWARD OUTWARD

Where do you look
When you cannot see

Who do you lean on
When there's no support

Which road do you take
When there are no signs

Each one a prop
Of support for the others

Hand in hands
For the good times and bad
The bonding within
Can never be broken
Its set for all time

THE FAMILY

MYRIAD

A tree may have
No branches removed

It may lose one
It may lose more

No matter how many
The tree remains

PROVERBIALS

Whatever road taken
Whichever path followed
It ends with a barrier
That is only raised
At the whim
Of the operator

Power is a glass wall
That is rarely scaled

A piece of string
Is as long
As the holder of the ball
Wants it to be

Blind sheep
Never sense
The cattle prod

Never put the rattle in the pram
It might be thrown back

Never point a finger
Without the nail polish

The rabbit hole
Goes as deep as the one
Who does the burrowing

Raising the curtain
Puts you on the stage

Why bother with rod and line
If there's enough people
To haul the net

You'll never know
What you missed
If you lost it
Or never had it
In the first place

FUN "N" GAMES

Irish shell game
You will need
1 dried pea
3 glass tumblers

General knowledge quiz
You will need
Clever bastards

Wrist and diddler
You will need
1. A well padlocked bedroom door
2. A reasonable excuse

The Irish riddle game
You will need
Irishmen
The players sit at a
Round table.
The player nearest
The floor goes first.
The first player
Composes a riddle
That nobody knows
The answer to.
He then passes the riddle
To the player on his left
The riddle is thus circulated
Around the table
The winner being the
First one to guess
The right answer

SQUEEGEE

Their parked in the bedroom corner
Just sitting there on the floor
Seems a bit pointless to keep them
We don't need the mop and bucket no more

Can't remember how many we got through
Just never kept up with the score
I suppose you could say it saves money
We don't need the mop and bucket no more

Does it really make any difference
Not needing the things anymore
Lets dump them into a skip
We don't need the mop and bucket no more

DIARY

Waves kiss the pages
Of a broken heart
Tears spell the epitaph
That tore it apart
Lines written
By an outstretched hand
None to receive
Or understand
The ebb signs the volume
Of the authors last word
Joined now forever
No one heard

PAIN

None spoke but all knew,
There's something about,
What friends are for
Silence is not always golden
The truth hurts
But it is the truth
None spoke but all knew.

PAIN II

All saw but did not see
There's something about going too far
Preying on a weakness
Is a weakness
All saw but did not see.

LOVE/HATE

How can two opposites
Turn out the same

How can two episodes
Have the same ending

How can two sides
Both lose the game

How can two words
Be opposed yet blended

DEMON

None to share
The silence of inner turmoil

None to listen
To the clammer within

None save receiver
On the same wavelength

None in the audience
But you

CATALOGUE

A motor car takes a wrong turn
An error to make the world burn
Failed assassin heading home
Oh Gavrilo didn't you know

Two shots fired a perfect score
Archduke and Sophie are no more
The coals were already aglow
Oh Gavrilo didn't you know

Dominoes toppled one by one
They could not be stopped once begun
Giving their all the lads did go
Oh Gavrilo didn't you know

Would it have happened without you
Had your aim not been straight and true
World war seeds your bullets did sew
Oh Gavrilo didn't you know

LADS

All over by Christmas
The tommies cried
Do our bit
Then wave goodbye

They didn't know
The ordeal before them
All sides machined
Dulce-Et-Decorum

Flanders, Ypres
Passchendaele, Somme
Never forget these places

Or the price paid so great
By the lads who went
With smiling faces

CIRCLE

The circle has a starting point
Where that point is
"Who can say?"

Who holds the compasses
Is it one hand or many

Do you stand at the tangent

Are you inside
Or do you forever follow the line
"Whos line"

PATORWELLISM

The friendly smile
The door that's always open
The shoulder squeeze
The listening ear
Is there something behind this
"Who decides"
Is it more subtle than Winston
A different version of a
Story with the same ending
"Concentrate"
Peer through the fog
"Look"
It's Orwell presenting O'Brien
George
You got it dead right

THE INVERTED POLITICAL TRIPOD

1	2	3
Fairness	Exploitation	Nationalism
Equality	Self interest	Segregation
Co-operation	Competition	Protectionism
Cannot	Cannot	Cannot
Function	Function	Function
With 2-3	With 1-3	With 1-2

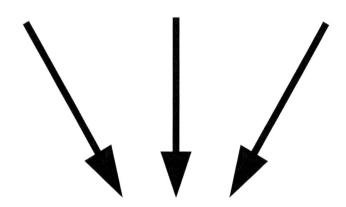

Eternal
Conflict

NATURE

Competition is innate
Systems amplify

WHAT IS LIFE

Life is for living
Life is good
Life is cruel
But, life is what
You make it
So enjoy life while you have it
Don't think of what people say
Because in the end they are
Only thinking of themselves
So enjoy life and laugh a lot,
Without laughter life's dull
And to be dull is sad
So enjoy life while you have it

R. A. Ward

Alan Ward

was born in Coventry in 1945.
He is married with one daughter
and his main interest is social history.
His poetry is based on relationship